Your Classroom Learning experience is just one part of the **New Ho**[...]
and valuable experience that includes Web-based resources during a[...]

The **New Horizons** learning solution includes online resources such [...]
tutorials, making it the finest and most robust learning environment a[...]

A full electronic version of the user manual - eCourseware - is available for reference and use post-class. Updates to the content within the eCourseware manual are automatic, providing you with access to the latest version of the course material at all times.

To access eCourseware and other online resources for this class, visit **www.newhorizons.com** and select **Student Resources**. **New Horizons Learning Port** a hosted, Web-based platform supports the delivery and management of your post-class resources. For more information about other available learning options, contact your local **New Horizons Computer Learning Center**.

Access Key: 7505-LPCLASS-2125

(Note: Access keys are case-sensitive and must be entered exactly as displayed.)

To access your online resources:

1. Go to the **New Horizons** homepage at **www.newhorizons.com**.
2. Click the **Student Resources** link on the lower left side of the **New Horizons** homepage.
3. Click on the **Learning Port** link to log in to the site.
4. Log in to the **Learning Port** using one of the options below:

Option 1: Returning User -- if you have an existing classroom **Learning Port** account, enter your Username and Password in the Registered Student area and click **Login**.

   a) Once you are successfully logged in to **Learning Port**, the homepage will display.
   b) Enter the **Access Key** box and click on **Send**.
   c) Your online learning resources will be added to your **Catalog**.

-OR-

Option 2: New User -- if you are a new classroom **Learning Port** user, you will need to complete the **Personal Information** form.

   a) Begin by clicking on the Enroll button. The **Access Key** box will display.
   b) Enter the **Access Key** in the **Access Key** box and click on **Send**.
   c) The **Personal Information** form will display. Enter your information and click on **Submit**.
      (Note: Remember to write down your Username and Password for future reference. This login will be used to access post class resources for current and future classes.)
   d) The student login page will display. Enter the Username and Password you created in your new student profile and click **Login**.
   e) Your online learning resources will be added to your **Catalog**.

Username: _____

Password: _____

This login provides access to class resources only. When creating your "Username" enter something unique such as adding the letters ILT (Instructor Led Training) to the end of the name. This will set it apart from logins that you may use for other types of online training.

Microsoft® Office Outlook® 2003– Level 1

Part Number: NH1690LGEEL
Course Edition: 1.1

ACKNOWLEDGMENTS

Project Team

Content Developer: Jeannine P. Pray • **Content Manager:** Cheryl Russo • **Content Editors:** J-P Altieri and Laura Thomas • **Material Editor:** Elizabeth M. Fuller • **Graphic/Print Designers:** Benjamin Northern and Isolina Salgado • **Project Technical Support:** Michael Toscano

NOTICES

DISCLAIMER: While Element K Content LLC takes care to ensure the accuracy and quality of these materials, we cannot guarantee their accuracy, and all materials are provided without any warranty whatsoever, including, but not limited to, the implied warranties of merchantability or fitness for a particular purpose. The name used in the data files for this course is that of a fictitious company. Any resemblance to current or future companies is purely coincidental. We do not believe we have used anyone's name in creating this course, but if we have, please notify us and we will change the name in the next revision of the course. Element K is an independent provider of integrated training solutions for individuals, businesses, educational institutions, and government agencies. Use of screenshots, photographs of another entity's products, or another entity's product name or service in this book is for editorial purposes only. No such use should be construed to imply sponsorship or endorsement of the book by, nor any affiliation of such entity with Element K. This courseware may contain links to sites on the Internet that are owned and operated by third parties (the "External Sites"). Element K is not responsible for the availability of, or the content located on or through, any External Site. Please contact Element K if you have any concerns regarding such links or External Sites.

TRADEMARK NOTICES: Element K and the Element K logo are trademarks of Element K LLC and its affiliates.

Microsoft® Outlook® 2003 is a registered trademark of Microsoft Corporation in the U.S. and other countries; the Microsoft Corporation products and services discussed or described may be trademarks of Microsoft Corporation. All other product names and services used throughout this course may be common law or registered trademarks of their respective proprietors.

Copyright © 2005 Element K Content LLC. All rights reserved. Screenshots used for illustrative purposes are the property of the software proprietor. This publication, or any part thereof, may not be reproduced or transmitted in any form or by any means, electronic or mechanical, including photocopying, recording, storage in an information retrieval system, or otherwise, without express written permission of Element K, 500 Canal View Boulevard, Rochester, NY 14623, (585) 240-7500, (800) 434-3466. Element K Courseware LLC's World Wide Web site is located at **www.elementkcourseware.com**.

This book conveys no rights in the software or other products about which it was written; all use or licensing of such software or other products is the responsibility of the user according to terms and conditions of the owner. Do not make illegal copies of books or software. If you believe that this book, related materials, or any other Element K materials are being reproduced or transmitted without permission, please call 1-800-478-7788.

This logo means that this courseware has been approved by the Microsoft® Office Specialist Program to be among the finest available for learning Microsoft Outlook 2003. It also means that upon completion of this courseware, you may be prepared to take an exam for Microsoft Offices Specialist qualification.

What is a Microsoft Office Specialist? A Microsoft Office Specialist is an individual who has passed exams for certifying his or her skills in one or more of the Microsoft Office desktop applications such as Microsoft Word, Microsoft Excel, Microsoft PowerPoint, Microsoft Outlook, Microsoft Access, or Microsoft Project. The Microsoft Office Specialist Program typically offers certification exams at the "Core" and "Expert" skill levels. The Microsoft Office Specialist Program is the only program in the world approved by Microsoft for testing proficiency in Microsoft Office desktop applications and Microsoft Project. This testing program can be a valuable asset in any job search or career advancement.

To learn more about becoming a Microsoft Office Specialist, visit **www.microsoft.com/officespecialist**. To learn more about other Microsoft Office Specialist approved courseware from Element K, visit **www.elementkcourseware.com**.

*The availability of Microsoft Office Specialist certification exams varies by application, application version, and language. Visit **www.microsoft.com/officespecialist** for exam availability.

Microsoft, the Microsoft Office Logo, PowerPoint, and Outlook are trademarks or registered trademarks of Microsoft Corporation in the United States and/or other countries, and the Microsoft Office Specialist Logo is used under license from owner.

Element K is independent from Microsoft Corporation, and not affiliated with Microsoft in any manner. This publication may be used in assisting students to prepare for a Microsoft Office Specialist exam. Neither Microsoft, its designated program administrator or courseware reviewer, nor Element K warrants that use of this publication will ensure passing the relevant exam.

MICROSOFT® OFFICE OUTLOOK® 2003- LEVEL 1

LESSON 1 - GETTING STARTED WITH OUTLOOK

- **A. Log On to Outlook** 2
  - Outlook 2
- **B. The Outlook Environment** 4
  - Microsoft Office Outlook 2003 Window 4
  - Item 5
  - Folder 6
- **C. Compose and Send a Simple Message** 8
  - Email 8
  - The Message Form 9
  - Email Addresses 9
- **D. Open a Message** 12
  - Message Symbols 12
- **E. Reply to a Message** 13
  - Reply Options 13
  - The InfoBar 13
- **F. Print a Message** 14
- **G. Delete a Message** 15

LESSON 2 - COMPOSING MESSAGES

- **A. Address a Message** 18
  - Address Book 18
  - Global Address List 19
- **B. Format a Message** 20
- **C. Check Spelling and Grammar** 20
  - AutoCorrect 20

Contents

    D. Attach a File 22
        Attachment 22
    E. Forward a Message 23

Lesson 3 - Managing Mail

    A. Open and Save an Attachment 26
    B. Flag a Message 27
    C. Create a Folder 28
    D. Move Messages to a Folder 28
    E. Copy Messages to Folders 29
    F. Delete a Folder 30

Lesson 4 - Scheduling Appointments

    A. The Outlook Calendar 32
        Calendar Entries 32
        Views 32
    B. Schedule an Appointment 34
        The Appointment Form 34
        Calendar Symbols 35
    C. Assign a Category to an Appointment 37
        Category 37
    D. Update Calendar Entries 39

Lesson 5 - Scheduling Meetings

    A. Schedule a Meeting 42
        The Meeting Scheduling Process 42
        The Meeting Form 43
        Meeting Resources 44

Contents

- B. Reply to a Meeting Request 47
- C. Propose a New Meeting Time 48
- D. Track Meeting Responses 48
- E. Update a Meeting Request 49
- F. Cancel a Meeting Request 50
- G. Print the Calendar 51

Lesson 6 - Managing Contacts

- A. Add a Contact 54
  - Contacts 54
  - The Contact Form 55
  - The Outlook Address Book 55
- B. Sort Contacts 57
  - Sort Order 57
- C. Find a Contact 58
- D. Generate a Map 59
- E. Edit a Contact 60
- F. Delete a Contact 60
- G. Print Contacts 61

Lesson 7 - Managing Tasks

- A. Create a Task 64
  - Task 64
  - The Task Form 65

Contents

    B. Edit a Task 66

    C. Update a Task 67

Lesson 8 - Using Notes

    A. Create a Note 70

    B. Edit a Note 71

    C. Copy a Note 71

Appendix A - Microsoft Office Specialist Program

Glossary 79

Index 81

ABOUT THIS COURSE

This course is the first in a series of three Microsoft® Office Outlook® courses. It will provide you with the skills you need to start sending and responding to email in Microsoft® Outlook® 2003, as well as maintaining your Calendar, scheduling meetings, and working with tasks and notes.

You are very busy these days. You can't keep up with all the correspondence, appointments, meetings, and tasks you need to accomplish. Therefore, it is essential to have a tool capable of keeping large amounts of information organized and at your fingertips. That tool is Outlook, and you can use it to effectively communicate electronically.

Course Description

Target Student

This course is designed for people with a basic understanding of Microsoft Windows who need to learn how to use Microsoft® Outlook® 2003 to compose and send email, schedule appointments and meetings, manage contact information and tasks, and use notes. This course is intended for persons interested in pursuing the Microsoft® Office Specialist certification for Outlook.

Course Prerequisites

This course assumes that you are familiar with using personal computers and have used a mouse and keyboard; basic typing skills are recommended. You should be comfortable in the Windows environment and be able to use Windows to manage information on your computer. Specifically, you should be able to: launch and close programs; navigate to information stored on the computer; and manage files and folders. The following courses are recommended, or you should have equivalent knowledge of:

- *Windows XP Professional – Level 1*
- *Windows XP Professional – Level 2*
- *Windows XP – Introduction*
- *Windows 2000 – Introduction*

How to Use This Book

As a Learning Guide

Each lesson covers one broad topic or set of related topics. Lessons are arranged in order of increasing proficiency with *Microsoft® Outlook® 2003*; skills you acquire in one lesson are used and developed in subsequent lessons. For this reason, you should work through the lessons in sequence.

We organized each lesson into results-oriented topics. Topics include all the relevant and supporting information you need to master *Microsoft® Outlook® 2003*, and activities allow you to apply this information to practical hands-on examples.

You get to try out each new skill on a specially prepared sample file. This saves you typing time and allows you to concentrate on the skill at hand. Through the use of sample files, hands-on activities, illustrations that give you feedback at crucial steps, and supporting background information, this book provides you with the foundation and structure to learn *Microsoft® Outlook® 2003* quickly and easily.

As a Review Tool

Any method of instruction is only as effective as the time and effort you are willing to invest in it. In addition, some of the information that you learn in class may not be important to you immediately, but it may become important later on. For this reason, we encourage you to spend some time reviewing the topics and activities after the course. For additional challenge when reviewing activities, try the What You Do column before looking at the How You Do It column.

As a Reference

The organization and layout of the book make it easy to use as a learning tool and as an after-class reference. You can use this book as a first source for definitions of terms, background information on given topics, and summaries of procedures.

Microsoft® Outlook® 2003 - Level 1 is one of a series of New Horizons courseware titles that addresses Microsoft® Office Specialist skill sets. The Office Specialist program is for individuals who use Microsoft's business desktop software and who seek recognition for their expertise with specific Microsoft products. Certification candidates must pass one or more product proficiency exams in order to earn Office Specialist certification.

Course Objectives

In this course, you will compose and send email, schedule appointments and meetings, manage contact information and tasks, and use notes.

You will:

- identify the components of the Outlook environment and compose and respond to a simple message.
- compose messages.
- use folders to manage mail.

- schedule appointments.
- schedule meetings.
- manage contacts and contact information.
- create and edit tasks.
- create and edit notes.

Lesson 1
Getting Started with Outlook

Lesson Time
40 minutes to 50 minutes

In this lesson, you will identify the components of the Outlook environment and compose and respond to a simple message.

You will:

- Log on to Outlook.
- List the components of the Outlook environment.
- Compose and send a simple message.
- Open a message.
- Reply to a message.
- Print a message.
- Delete a message.

LESSON 1

Introduction

Many of us have to handle large amounts of business communications, including correspondence. Therefore, the logical place to start in Microsoft® Office Outlook® 2003 is with mail. In this lesson, you will create and respond to a mail message.

You are working your way through stacks of correspondence. Wouldn't it be great if there was a more effective way to correspond with others? By using Outlook, you can compose, send, and reply to messages quickly and easily, enabling you to efficiently and effectively handle your correspondence.

TOPIC A

Log On to Outlook

Before you can use Outlook, you need to log on so that Outlook recognizes you as an authorized user. In this topic, you will log on to Outlook.

Just as you might need to follow a process to access resources within an office building, you need to follow a log on process to access Outlook. Once you are logged on, you can begin communicating electronically with others.

Outlook

Definition:

> Outlook is a software program that includes email, the Calendar, Contacts, the Tasks list, Notes, and the Journal that you can use to electronically communicate with others and manage personal information.

Example:

> Figure 1-1 displays examples of how you can use Outlook to communicate electronically.

LESSON 1

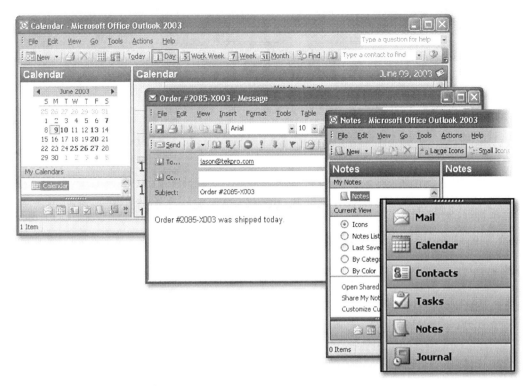

Figure 1-1: *Outlook tasks.*

How to Log On to Outlook

Procedure Reference: Log On to Outlook

To log on to Outlook:

1. On the Windows taskbar, click Start. The Start menu is displayed.

2. Choose All Programs→Microsoft Office→Microsoft Office Outlook 2003. The Connect To dialog box is displayed.

3. In the Password text box, enter your password.

4. Click OK. Outlook is opened.

5. In the upper-right corner of the window, click the Maximize button.

Lesson 1

Topic B

The Outlook Environment

Your first step when working with Outlook is to determine how it works. By understanding the basics of the software, you will have a solid foundation upon which to build toward more critical skills. In this topic, you will explore the Outlook application and identify window components.

When you need to use an item for the first time, it's important to become familiar with the item's components before you start using it. The same is true for Outlook. By knowing the components of Outlook, it will be easier to use and you will be able to work more efficiently because you are familiar with the environment.

Microsoft Office Outlook 2003 Window

After you log on, the Microsoft Office Outlook 2003 window is displayed. Its components are listed in the following table.

Component	What It Does
Title bar	Displays the name of the current folder and the application.
Menu bar	Lists the menus.
Ask A Question box	Provides a place to enter questions.
Standard toolbar	Provides quick access to some of the most frequently used commands.
Navigation Pane	The column on the left side of the window that provides access to all components of Outlook.
Task pane	Provides a window that you can use to access commonly used commands.
Go Menu	Part of the Navigation Pane that allows you to quickly switch between components.
Quick Launch bar	Part of the Navigation Pane that provides quick access to frequently used components.
Reading Pane	Displays the contents of the selected message without opening the message.
Status bar	Displays information about the active folder.

Figure 1-2 displays the components of the Microsoft Office Outlook 2003 window.

Lesson 1

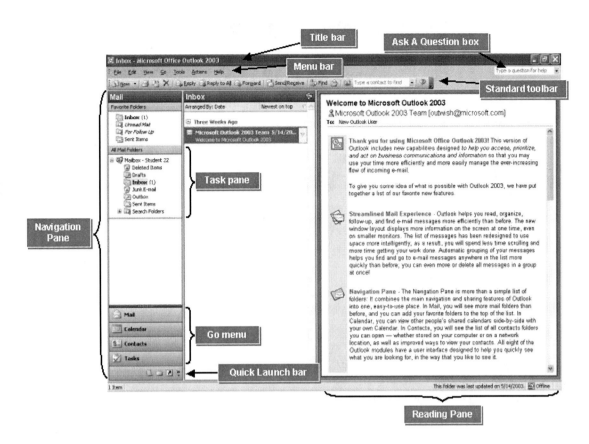

Figure 1-2: *The components of the Microsoft Office Outlook 2003 window.*

Item

Definition:

An *item* is a basic element created in Outlook that holds information and is stored in a specific location.

Example:

Figure 1-3 displays an example of an item in Outlook.

Lesson 1

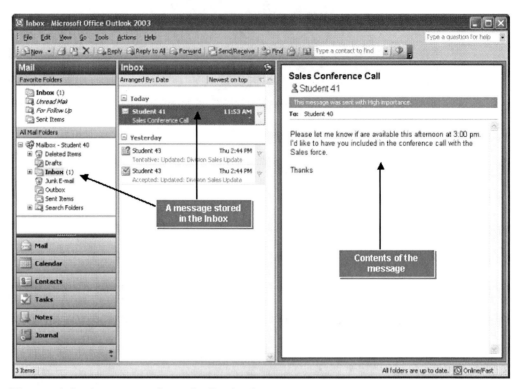

Figure 1-3: *A message item in Outlook.*

Outlook Items

Items in Outlook include:

- Messages
- Appointments
- Meetings
- Contacts
- Tasks
- Notes

Folder

Definition:

A *folder* is a tool that you can use to store and organize Outlook items.

Example:

Figure 1-4 displays an example of a folder in Outlook.

LESSON 1

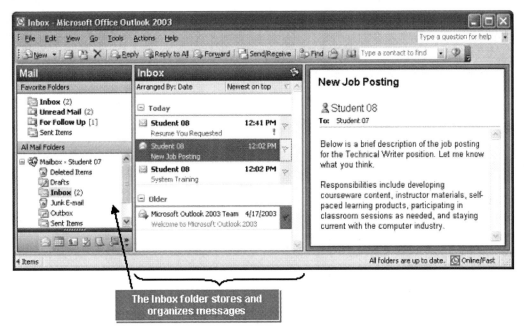

Figure 1-4: *A folder in Outlook.*

The Outlook Environment

Outlook contains six main components that you can use to communicate with others. These components are folders and are listed in the following table.

Component	Description
Inbox	Where you send and receive messages.
Calendar	Where you schedule appointments, meetings, and events.
Contacts	Where you enter and track business and personal contacts.
Tasks List	Where you create and manage tasks.
Notes	Where you quickly record reminders.
Journal	Where you can automatically track all items that you have specified as they occur.

Additional Outlook Folders

Additional folders in Outlook include:

- Deleted Items—Stores any items that you delete in Outlook.
- Drafts—Stores copies of unfinished messages you can complete and send at a later time.
- Junk E-mail—Contains junk email messages.
- Outbox—Temporarily stores messages you send until they are delivered.
- Sent Items—Stores copies of messages you send to others.
- Sync Issues—Contains all of the synchronization logs.

- Search Folders—Contain views of mail items that satisfy specific search criteria.

Help

While you're using Outlook, you can use the following resources if you need help:
- The Type A Question For Help box located on the Menu bar.
- Microsoft Outlook Help task pane, which you can display by choosing Help→ Microsoft Outlook Help.

TOPIC C

Compose and Send a Simple Message

You are familiar with Outlook and the environment, and you're ready to start communicating. In this topic, you will compose and send mail messages.

You need to send some important information to a client who is located in another part of the country. The client needs the information today. Sending it by regular mail is not an option. The client is out of the office, so you can't call him either. By using Outlook, you can quickly and efficiently send the information in a simple message.

Email

Electronic mail, or *email*, is an application that allows a user to create, send, and receive electronic messages. You can send information and receive information from users within your network of computers or outside your network of computers via the Internet.

Figure 1-5 displays an example of the flow of email.

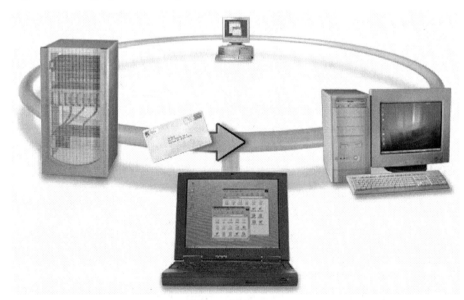

Figure 1-5: *The flow of email inside a network of computers and via the Internet.*

Lesson 1

The Message Form

When you create a new message, Outlook displays a Message form that contains text boxes in which you can enter specific information. The four main text boxes in a Message form are listed in Table 1-1.

Table 1-1: *Message Form Text Boxes*

Text Box	Information to Enter
To	Email address or user name of the person to whom you want to send the message.
Cc	Email address or user name of anyone who you want to receive a copy of the message (Carbon Copy).
Subject	A brief description of the message.
Message Body	The text of the message.

Figure 1-6 displays an example of a completed Message form.

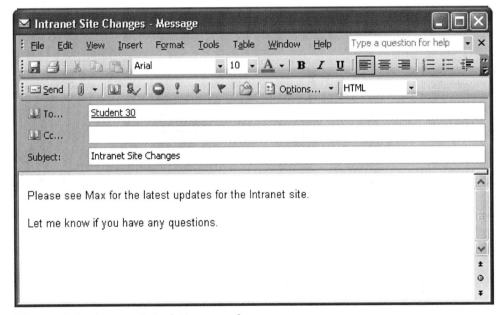

Figure 1-6: *A completed Message form.*

Default Mail Editor

Microsoft Word is the default mail editor for Outlook. Therefore, when you create mail messages, you will have access to a number of Word features, making it easier to create messages in Outlook.

Email Addresses

Definition:

An *email address* is a string used to specify the user name and location where users can send you email.

Lesson 1

Example:

Figure 1-7 displays some examples of email addresses.

Figure 1-7: *Examples of email addresses.*

How to Compose and Send a Message

Procedure Reference: Compose and Send a Message

To compose and send a new message:

1. On the Standard toolbar, click New. A new Message form is displayed.

2. In the To text box, type the name of the user to whom you want to address the message.

    > If you are addressing the message to more than one recipient, separate the user names with a semicolon (;).

    > In the To text box, an underlined user name indicates that it matches a name on the server.

    > Although most messages will contain a subject and some text in the message body, only the To text box must be filled in to send a message.

3. Click in the Subject field.

4. Enter a subject of your choice.

5. Press Tab to move to the message body text box.

6. Enter a message.

7. If desired, press Enter twice and type your name.

8. On the Standard toolbar, click Send to send the message.

    > When the message arrives at its destination, a message alert is displayed briefly in the lower-right corner of the Outlook window. It contains the sender's name, the subject, and the first few words of the message.

Email Etiquette

Net etiquette, or Network etiquette, is a set of guidelines for ethical behavior on the Internet, including sending and receiving email. You can become a responsible Internet citizen by applying the guidelines outlined in the following list.

- Think twice before clicking the Send button. Once you send an email message, you might not be able to take it back.

- Realize that an email message can be easily circulated (forwarded, printed and distributed, and so on).
- Be cautious with humor and sarcasm. Statements that are funny person-to-person might lose their humor in writing and appear, instead, confusing or even vicious.
- Use emoticons (emotion icons), or smileys, to convey subtle emotional tones that cannot be adequately expressed in written words. The following table displays a few of the emoticons (look at them sideways):

Emoticon	Conveys
:-)	Cheeriness
;-)	Light sarcasm (a wink)
:-(	Displeasure or sadness
:-()	Alarm
:~?	Confusion
:-D	Laughter
:-I	Boredom or indifference
:-o	Surprise

- Use smileys sparingly; they can be tedious to read.
- Avoid typing in all uppercase letters when emphasizing words—it seems like shouting.
- Never send unsolicited advertisements to email recipients or newsgroups. This is called *spamming*, and it's a serious Internet offense.
- Keep the line length of your message or posting to 60 or fewer characters. Some users' screens cannot display more than 60 characters per line.
- Use descriptive subjects so that your messages are easier to find and file.
- Follow a newsgroup's discussions for a while to familiarize yourself with its objectives and general tone before you begin posting articles. This technique is called lurking; posting your first message is called delurking.
- Read the FAQs (Frequently Asked Questions) of a newsgroup before you start posting articles. Most groups have FAQs for new subscribers.
- Post your test articles to a test group, such as alt.test or misc.test. Posting tests to non-test newsgroups is considered rude.
- Take a moment to decide whether it's more appropriate to respond privately to an individual's post in a mailing list or newsgroup than to respond publicly to the whole list or group.
- Don't engage in rampant *flaming* (responding harshly or insultingly to an email or posting). Flame wars can be very ugly.

Net etiquette is a serious topic. If you post inappropriate material—unsolicited advertisements, inflammatory or insulting remarks, misinformation, and so on—to mailing lists or newsgroups, there is a good chance you'll be flamed publicly (in newsgroup postings) or privately (in email). In extreme cases, Net etiquette violators can be banished from a mailing list or newsgroup.

Lesson 1

Save Messages

While composing a message, you might decide that you are not ready to send the message. You can save a message and send it at a later time by choosing File→Save. The message is stored in the Drafts folder. When you're ready to finish the message, simply open the message, add the desired information to the Message form, and send the message.

Topic D
Open a Message

You know how to compose and send messages. But, what will you do when someone else sends you a message? In this topic, you will open a message.

Your Inbox contains an important message from a client for which you have been waiting. Unless you open the message, you won't know what the contents of the message include.

Message Symbols

Each message in your Inbox displays with one or more message symbols next to it. The symbols represent the type or status of the message.

Examples of Message Symbols

Table 1-2 displays message symbols.

Table 1-2: *Message Symbols*

Symbol	Description
❗	High importance message
⬇	Low importance message
📖	A read message
✉	An unread message
↩	A replied message
↪	A forwarded message
📎	Message has an attachment
🚩	Message is flagged for follow-up
✓	Message is flagged as complete

How to Open a Message

Procedure Reference: Open a Message

To open a message:

1. In the Inbox, open a message.
   - Double-click the message you want to open.

Lesson 1

- Select the message you want to open and choose File→Open→Selected Items.
- Right-click the message you want to open and choose Open.
- Select the message you want to open and press Enter.

You don't have to open a message to read it. You can read the contents of a message by using the Reading Pane.

Topic E

Reply to a Message

You have created, sent, and received email messages. What if you receive an email that requires you to reply? In this topic, you will open and respond to messages in your Inbox.

A co-worker sent you a message asking for feedback on a proposed agenda for an upcoming meeting. Unless you respond to him, he won't know what you think about the proposed agenda.

Reply Options

When you want to reply to a message, you have a few options.

- Use the *Reply* option to send a response to the sender of the message.
- Use the *Reply To All* option to send a response to the sender and copies of the response to anyone who received the original message.
- Use the *Forward* option to forward a copy of the message to someone who did not receive the original message.

The InfoBar

The InfoBar displays information about what has occurred or what action you need to take. It is displayed below the active toolbar. Figure 1-8 displays an example of the InfoBar.

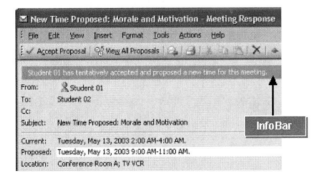

Figure 1-8: *An example of the InfoBar.*

Lesson 1: Getting Started with Outlook

Lesson 1

How to Reply to a Message

Procedure Reference: Reply to a Message

To reply to an open message:

1. On the Standard toolbar, click Reply to display a Message form.

   > The To and Subject text boxes are automatically filled in and information from the original message is inserted in the message body text box.

2. In the message body text box, enter the text of the message.
3. Send the message.

   > You don't have to open a message to reply to it. Simply select the message in the Inbox and, on the Standard toolbar, click Reply.

Topic F

Print a Message

Although an advantage of email is that it doesn't require paper, there will be occasions when you will want to have a hard copy of a message, either one you've sent or one you've received. In this topic, you will print a copy of a message.

A co-worker sent you the final meeting agenda in a message. Some of the agenda items are your responsibility. By printing a copy of the message, you will have a hard copy of the agenda for reference and portability, so you can easily prepare for the meeting.

How to Print a Message

Procedure Reference: Print a Message

To print a message:

1. Open the message you want to print.
2. Choose File→Print to display the Print dialog box.
3. To increase the number of copies you want to print, in the Number Of Copies spin box, click the up arrow as needed to enter the appropriate number of copies.
4. If necessary, modify the desired print options.
5. Click Print to print the message.
6. Close the message.

   > If you want to print a message by using the default print options, you don't have to open the message. On the Standard toolbar, simply click the Print button.

Topic G

Delete a Message

Once you start using Outlook to communicate electronically, your Inbox might fill up quickly with messages. In this topic, you will delete messages that you no longer need.

You have been using Outlook for a while, so your Inbox contains a lot of old messages that you no longer need. By deleting those old messages, your Inbox will be less cluttered and you will save space on your hard drive.

How to Delete a Message

Procedure Reference: Delete a Message

To delete a message:

1. With the message selected or opened that you want to delete, click the Delete button.
2. If necessary, verify the deletion of a message:
    a. In the All Mail Folders pane, click the plus sign (+) to expand your mailbox.
    b. Select the Deleted Items folder.

Recover Deleted Messages

After you delete a message, you can recover it from the Deleted Items folder.

- Drag the message from the Deleted Items folder to any other folder.
- Choose Edit→Undo Delete.

  ⚠ This option only works immediately after deleting a message.

Lesson 1 Follow-up

Nice work! Now that you can identify the basic components of Outlook and you've sent and responded to email messages, you're ready to move ahead to the next step.

1. **What did you find most helpful about the Outlook environment? Why?**

   Answers will vary.

2. **What did you find most confusing about the Outlook environment? Why?**

   Answers will vary.

Notes

LESSON 2
Composing Messages

Lesson Time
50 minutes to 60 minutes

In this lesson, you will compose messages.

You will:
- Address a message by using the Global Address List.
- Format a message.
- Check the spelling and grammar in a message.
- Attach a file to a message.
- Forward a message.

Lesson 2

Introduction

You have created and responded to some basic messages. The longer you use Outlook, you will need to know how to create more detailed messages. In this lesson, you will create messages that include formatting, are error-free, and include information from other sources.

Before you send a message, you might find it necessary to alter its contents. Perhaps you want to emphasize some text within the body of the message or correct a misspelled word. Outlook provides you with tools to ensure that your messages are both accurate and easy to read.

Topic A

Address a Message

So far, you've sent mail messages where you knew the recipient's name and email address. What if you don't know the correct spelling of a person's name or their email address? In this topic, you will use an Outlook tool to accurately address email messages.

You need to send a get well card to a co-worker; however, you've forgotten her street address. Therefore, you use the phone book to ensure you have the correct address. Similar to a phone book, you can use an Outlook Address Book to quickly address an electronic message and ensure that the address of the recipient is correct.

Address Book

Definition:

The *Address Book* is a collection of address books or address lists that you can use to find and select names, email addresses, and distribution lists to quickly address messages.

Example:

Figure 2-1 displays an example of the Address Book.

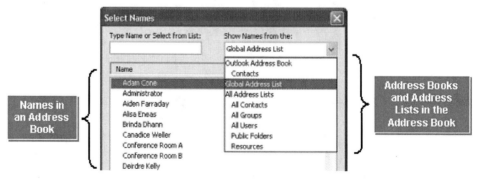

Figure 2-1: *An example of the Address Book.*

Global Address List

Definition:
The *Global Address List* is a list of all user names and global distribution lists in a particular organization that is created and maintained by the Microsoft Exchange Server Administrator. You can only access the Global Address List if you are using a Microsoft Exchange Server email account.

Example:
Figure 2-2 displays an example of a Global Address List.

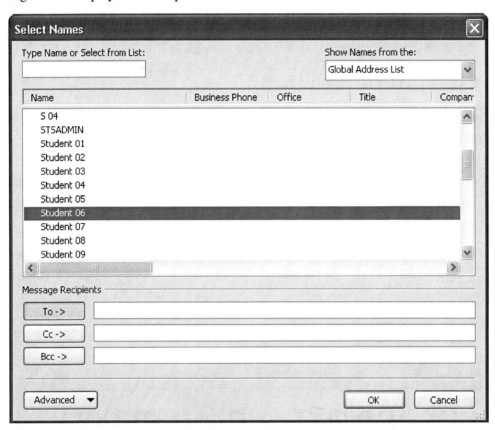

Figure 2-2: *The contents of a Global Address List.*

How to Address a Message

Procedure Reference: Address a Message

To address a message by using the Global Address List:

1. Display a new Message form.
2. To the left of the To text box, click To to display the Select Names dialog box.
3. In the list box, select the user name of the person to whom you want to address the message.
4. In the Message Recipients section, click To to place the selected user name in the To text box.
5. Click OK.

Lesson 2

Topic B

Format a Message

You have composed a message that contains text that you would like to make more distinctive. One way you can do that is to change the formatting of the text. In this topic, you will format a message.

You need to send a message that contains important dates and times for some upcoming events. You want to make sure that the dates and times stand out in the message text. By formatting specific text in a message, you will emphasize that text, drawing the reader's attention to it.

How to Format a Message

Procedure Reference: Format a Message

To format a message:

1. Select the text that you want to emphasize.

   To select all the message text, press Ctrl+A or choose Edit→Select All.

2. Apply the format.
   - On the Standard toolbar, click the appropriate button.
   - Choose Format and the appropriate formatting menu option.

Topic C

Check Spelling and Grammar

Because the messages you already sent were basic, you weren't too worried about your spelling and grammar when you sent them. However, eventually, you will compose messages where accurate spelling and grammar will be essential. In this topic, you will check the spelling and grammar of a message.

Whenever you're typing, there's always the possibility of making an error. For example, you know the correct spelling of the word "their," but somehow it always comes out "thier" when you type it. When you are trying to convey a professional image, misspelled words and incorrect grammar can make you look unprofessional. With Outlook, you can ensure that there are no misspellings or incorrect grammar in your messages.

AutoCorrect

The AutoCorrect feature detects common typing mistakes, including misspelled words, grammar problems, incorrect capitalization, and common typos, and either automatically corrects them or brings them to your attention. By default, the AutoCorrect feature is on.

Lesson 2

How to Check Spelling and Grammar

Procedure Reference: Check Spelling and Grammar

By default, spelling and grammar are automatically checked when you type a message. Wavy red underlines indicate a possible spelling error. Wavy green underlines indicate a possible error in grammar.

To check the spelling and grammar of a message all at once:

1. Choose Tools→Spelling And Grammar. The Spelling And Grammar dialog box is displayed.

    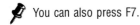 You can also press F7.

2. Correct any words that Outlook does not recognize.
   - Click Ignore Once to skip the current occurrence of the word.
   - Click Ignore All to skip all occurrences of the word.
   - Click Add To Dictionary to keep the word unchanged and add the word to the user dictionary.
   - Click Change after you change the spelling of the word by either entering a different spelling or selecting a word from the Suggestions list.
   - Click Change All to change the spelling of all instances of the same word.

3. If a spelling and grammar error is found and corrected, click Yes to continue checking the remainder of the document.

4. Click OK to close the message box.

Recall a Message

You can recall, or take back, a sent message if the message meets the following criteria:

- It has not been opened by the recipient.
- It has not been moved from the Inbox.
- The recipient is running Outlook and is logged on.

To recall a message:

1. Display the contents of the Sent Items folder.
2. Open the message you want to recall.
3. Choose Actions→Recall This Message.
4. In the Recall This Message dialog box, verify that Delete Unread Copies Of This Message is selected.
5. Click OK.
6. If you want to replace the message, create and send a new message.

Lesson 2: Composing Messages

Topic D

Attach a File

When you create a message, you might have information you want to include, but you don't want to retype that information in the message body. In this topic, you will attach a file to a message.

You have some information in a separate file that you want to include in a message. Retyping that information in the message will take some time. You can't copy and paste the information, because it's in a different file format. By attaching the file to your message, you can include the additional information without wasting time adding the information to your message.

Attachment

Definition:

An *attachment* is a copy of any type of file or an Outlook item that you can add to an Outlook item and then separate from the Outlook item.

Example:

Figure 2-3 displays an example of an attachment and the contents of the attachment in its associated application.

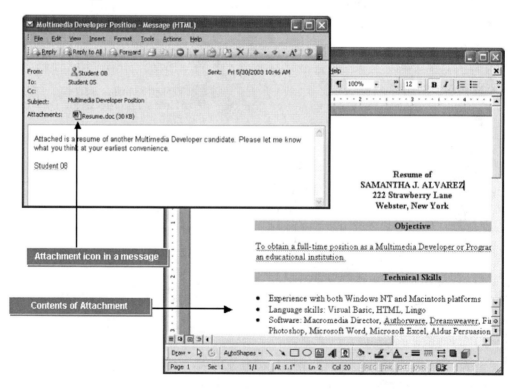

Figure 2-3: *An example of an attachment.*

File Type and Size

There are a few file type and size guidelines you should follow before attaching files or items to an Outlook item.

- Make sure the recipient of an attachment will be able to open and read the attachment. The recipient must have the application in which the attachment was created or a similar application.
- Be aware of attachment size, as a large attachment will use a lot of space and might delay the opening of the item to which it is attached.

How to Attach a File

Procedure Reference: Attach a File to a Message

To attach a file to a message:

1. On the E-mail toolbar, click the Insert File button. The Insert File dialog box is displayed.
2. Select the file you want to attach.
   - Double-click the file you want to attach.
   - Select the file you want to attach and click Insert.

> An attachment in a message that is formatted as HTML or Plain Text displays in a text box below the Subject text box. An attachment in a message that is formatted as Rich Text, or any other items, is included in the body of the item.

> After you send a message, sometimes the recipient has to wait a few moments for the message to display in the Inbox. To refresh the Inbox and display any incoming messages, you can click the Send/Receive button.

TOPIC E

Forward a Message

You have received messages and sent responses directly to the original sender of the message. But what if you want to send the message to someone who wasn't an original recipient? In this topic, you will forward a message.

You received a message from a co-worker that you want to share with another co-worker who didn't receive the original message. By forwarding the message, you can quickly and easily share the information. The only information that you need to enter is the recipient's email address.

How to Forward a Message

Procedure Reference: Forward a Message

To forward a message:

1. If necessary, open the message you want to forward.
2. On the Standard toolbar, click Forward. A new Message form is displayed.

Lesson 2

3. Address the message to the appropriate recipients.
4. If desired, enter a message.
5. Send the message.
6. Close the original message.

Lesson 2 Follow-up

Congratulations! You've created several email messages by using a variety of options. The Global Address List will come in handy when you're not sure how to spell someone's name. You can make your messages look more professional by formatting them and checking their spelling and grammar. You will also be more efficient by attaching files and forwarding messages.

1. **Now that you know how to spell check an email message, do you think you will use that feature regularly? Why or why not?**

    Answers will vary.

2. **What types of formatting do you think you will use in your email messages?**

    Answers will vary.

LESSON 3
Managing Mail

Lesson Time
50 minutes to 60 minutes

In this lesson, you will use folders to manage mail.

You will:

- Save an attachment.
- Flag a message.
- Create a folder.
- Move messages to a folder.
- Copy messages to multiple folders.
- Delete a folder.

Lesson 3

Introduction

You have sent and received several messages, and your Inbox is starting to fill up. In this lesson, you will do some housekeeping to keep your messages organized and easier to find.

Your mailbox is overflowing. There are many messages you've received and want to keep yet others you no longer need. It's becoming more difficult to find certain messages. By organizing your mailbox, it will be easier to retrieve information efficiently.

Topic A

Open and Save an Attachment

You already know how to attach a file to a message and send it to someone. There will be times when you will receive a mail message that contains an attachment, and you will need to know what to do with the attached file. In this topic, you will save an attachment.

You received a message that contains an attachment. You have read the message, but you don't have time to review the contents of the attachment. By saving the attachment, you can refer to it later at a more convenient time. Also, you can then delete the message that you no longer need, saving space in your Inbox.

How to Open and Save an Attachment

Procedure Reference: Open an Attachment

To open an attachment:

1. Open the message that contains the attachment you want to open.
2. On the Attachments line of the Message form, double-click the name of the attachment to open the Opening Mail Attachment dialog box.
3. Click Open to open the file in the associated application. A message box is displayed.
4. Click OK to close the message box.

Procedure Reference: Save an Attachment

To save an attachment:

1. If necessary, open the message that contains the attachment you want to save.
2. Choose File→Save Attachments to display the Save Attachment dialog box.
3. If necessary, navigate to the folder location of your choice.
4. In the File Name text box, enter a name for the attachment.
5. Click Save.
6. Close the message.

> To delete an attachment, open the message that contains the attachment you want to delete. In the Attachments text box, select the attachment and click the Delete button.

Topic B

Flag a Message

Some of the messages that you receive you will want to refer to later. By flagging a message, you can draw your attention to it. In this topic, you will flag a message.

You received a message that contains information that you will need to refer to in a few weeks. Because you have so many other messages in your Inbox, you're concerned that you will forget to revisit that particular message at the appropriate time. By flagging the message, it will stand out, drawing your attention to it. The flag will ensure that the message is easy to find and is a reminder to refer back to the message.

How to Flag a Message

Procedure Reference: Flag a Message for Follow-up

To flag a message for follow-up:

1. Right-click the message you want to flag and choose Follow Up→Add Reminder to display the Flag For Follow Up dialog box.

   In an open message, you can click the Follow Up button on the Standard toolbar.

2. Click the Due By drop-down arrow. A pop-up Calendar is displayed.

3. Select the date on which you need to follow up.

4. Click OK.

   When a flagged message is due for follow-up, the text in the message header will change from black to red.

5. If necessary, confirm that the message is marked for follow-up.

Mark a Message Unread

You can manually change the status of a message from read to unread.

1. In the Inbox, either select or open the message you want to mark as unread.

2. Choose Edit→Mark As Unread.

In the Inbox, the message is now bold and has a closed envelope symbol, indicating an unread message.

Lesson 3

Topic C

Create a Folder

Your Inbox contains many messages. It would be easier to find messages if they were stored in an organized manner. In this topic, you will create folders.

You have many messages in your Inbox that pertain to a variety of subjects. You need to re-read those messages that pertain to the upcoming job fair. It's going to take some time to locate all the messages you need. If your Inbox was organized so that all the messages that pertain to the job fair were together, your job would be so much easier.

How to Create a Folder

Procedure Reference: Create a Folder

To create a folder:

1. On the New Mail Message button, click the drop-down arrow. A drop-down menu is displayed.
2. From the expanded drop-down menu, choose Folder to display the Create New Folder dialog box.
3. In the Name text box, enter the name of the folder.
4. If necessary, in the Select Where To Place The Folder list box, select the location where you want to create the folder.
5. Click OK.

Topic D

Move Messages to a Folder

Your messages arrive in your Inbox, but they don't have to remain there. You created some new folders to better organize your messages. In this topic, you will transfer messages from one folder to another.

You created a folder to store all messages related to the job fair. Now, you need to move all the job fair messages to that new folder. After the messages are moved, your Inbox will be less cluttered and all the job fair messages will be in one place, easy to refer to when necessary.

How to Move Messages to a Folder

Procedure Reference: Move Messages to a Folder

To move messages to a folder:

1. Select the message you want to move.

2. On the Standard toolbar, click the Move To Folder button. A drop-down list is displayed.

3. Select the folder to which you want to move the message.

4. If necessary, in the All Mail Folders pane of the Navigation Pane, select the folder to which you moved the message to confirm that your message has been moved.

TOPIC E
Copy Messages to Folders

You might receive messages that contain information on more than one subject. It would make organizing more efficient if you could save those messages in more than one folder. In this topic, you will copy messages to multiple folders.

You received a message that contains information on two different subjects. Because the message refers to multiple subjects, you're not sure how to organize your Inbox so that you can find the information when you need it. By copying the message, the information it contains can be stored in multiple folders with other similar information.

How to Copy Messages to a Folder

Procedure Reference: Copy Messages to a Folder

To copy a message to a folder:

1. Select the message you want to copy.

2. Choose Edit→Copy.

3. In the All Mail Folders pane, select the folder to which you want to copy the message.

4. Choose Edit→Paste to paste the copied message to the selected folder.

Lesson 3: Managing Mail

LESSON 3

TOPIC F

Delete a Folder

Inboxes tend to fill up very quickly with messages and folders. Before you know it, you have dozens of old items that you no longer need. In this topic, you will delete folders.

You created a folder to store the messages for a particular project. The project is complete and you no longer need the folder or its contents. By deleting the folder, you will save space and your Inbox will be easier to manage because it won't contain unnecessary information.

How to Delete a Folder

Procedure Reference: Delete a Folder

> To delete a folder:
>
> 1. In the All Mail Folders pane, select the folder you want to delete.
> 2. On the Standard toolbar, click the Delete button.
> 3. In the message box, click Yes to confirm the deletion of the selected folder.

Lesson 3 Follow-up

Congratulations! You now know how to keep your mailbox organized so that you can access and retrieve messages efficiently. You know how to work with attachments and flag messages for easy reference. You can create folders and move and copy messages to suit your needs. In addition, you can also delete folders that are no longer needed.

1. **List some reasons you might flag a message.**

    Answers will vary.

2. **What folders could you create to better organize your messages?**

    Answers will vary.

LESSON 4
Scheduling Appointments

Lesson Time
30 minutes to 40 minutes

In this lesson, you will schedule appointments.

You will:

- List the components of the Outlook Calendar.
- Schedule an appointment.
- Assign a category to an appointment.
- Update Calendar entries.

Lesson 4

Introduction

You have discovered how Outlook helps you communicate electronically and manage those communications. You can also keep your schedule organized electronically by using the Calendar. In this lesson, you will use the Calendar to manage your appointments.

Your paper calendar is a mess. You've scheduled, rescheduled, and cancelled appointments. There are scribbled notes posted on certain days as reminders. By using the Outlook Calendar, your schedule will always be up to date and easy to read.

Topic A

The Outlook Calendar

Before you use the Calendar, you will need to become familiar with its components and how they work. By understanding the basics of the Calendar, you will have a solid foundation upon which to build more critical skills. In this topic, you will explore the Outlook Calendar and identify its components.

After logging on to Outlook for the first time, you familiarized yourself with the Outlook environment. Before using the Calendar, it's important to familiarize yourself with it. By knowing the components of the Calendar, it will be easier to use and you will be able to work more efficiently because you are familiar with it.

Calendar Entries

There are different types of entries that you can create in your Calendar. Those entry types are listed in the following table.

Entry Type	Used To
Appointment	Reserve a time slot once for a designated purpose.
Recurring Appointment	Reserve a time slot more than once for a designated purpose.
Event	Reserve a specific day or group of days for a designated purpose.
Meeting Request	Reserve a time slot once for a designated purpose involving other participants.
Recurring Meeting Request	Reserve a time slot more than once for a designated purpose involving other participants.

Views

Definition:

A *view* is a way to display items in an Outlook folder.

Lesson 4

Example:

Figure 4-1 displays an example of a Calendar view.

Figure 4-1: *An example of the Month view.*

Calendar Views

Items on your Calendar can be viewed in several ways. The most common Calendar views are listed in the following table.

View	Displays
Day	A detailed schedule for one day, divided in hourly time slots.
Work Week	The five work days (Monday through Friday) divided in hourly time slots.
Week	The entire week (Monday through Sunday) where each day is represented by a box with no time slots.
Month	An entire month with no time slots.

The Outlook Calendar

The Calendar consists of two main components.

- The *Appointment Section* is divided into hourly time slots and displays all appointments for that day.
- The *Date Navigator* consists of Calendars for two adjacent months that you can use to quickly select a date to display or add items.

Figure 4-2 displays the components of the Outlook Calendar.

Lesson 4: Scheduling Appointments

Lesson 4

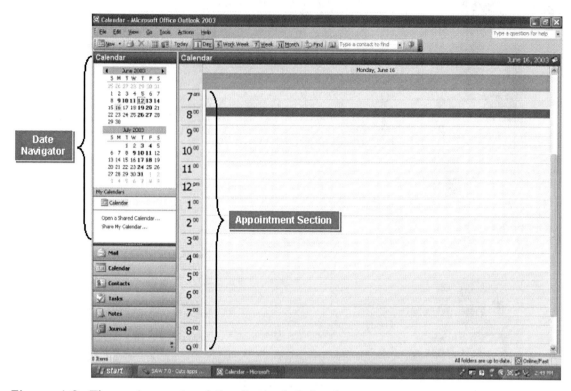

Figure 4-2: *The components of the Outlook Calendar.*

Topic B

Schedule an Appointment

You have used paper calendars to keep track of your schedule. Your Outlook Calendar allows you to perform the same functions as a paper calendar and more. In this topic, you will add an appointment to your Outlook Calendar.

A new client invites you to discuss their first project over lunch tomorrow. You accept the invitation, but you don't bother writing it down because you're sure you'll remember it. When you return from lunch the next day, you find a note on your desk from your manager asking you why you didn't show up for a meeting you had agreed to with him. How could you forget the meeting? By using the Outlook Calendar to track your time, you can avoid this type of predicament in the future.

The Appointment Form

When you create a new appointment, Outlook displays an Appointment form that contains text boxes in which you can enter specific information. Some of the text boxes in an Appointment form are listed in Table 4-1.

Lesson 4

Table 4-1: *Appointment Form Text Boxes*

Text Box	Information to Enter
Subject	A brief description of the appointment.
Location	Where the appointment will be held.
Start Time	The date and time the appointment starts.
End Time	The date and time the appointment ends.
Reminder	A reminder that notifies you when it's almost time for the appointment.
Show Time As	How the appointment should be displayed on your Calendar.
Label	What type of appointment it is.
Message Area	A place to enter any additional information about the appointment.

Figure 4-3 displays an example of a completed Appointment form.

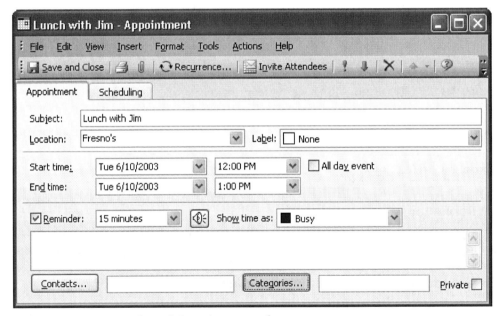

Figure 4-3: *A completed Appointment form.*

Calendar Symbols

To make it easier to determine at a glance what is on your Calendar, items on your Calendar are displayed with symbols.

Examples of Message Symbols

Some frequently used symbols are listed in Table 4-2.

Table 4-2: *Symbols Used in the Outlook Calendar*

Symbol	Meaning
	This appointment has a reminder.
	This is a recurring appointment.

Lesson 4: Scheduling Appointments

Lesson 4

Symbol	Meaning
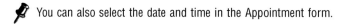	This is a meeting that involves multiple participants.

How to Schedule an Appointment

Procedure Reference: Schedule an Appointment

To schedule an appointment:

1. In the Date Navigator, select the date of the appointment.

    You can also select the date and time in the Appointment form.

2. On the Standard toolbar, click the New Appointment button to display a new Appointment form.

3. In the Subject field, enter a subject of your choice.

4. Press Tab to move to the Location field.

5. In the Location field, enter a location of your choice.

6. From the Start Time drop-down list, select the appropriate starting time of the appointment.

7. From the End Time drop-down list, select the appropriate ending time of the appointment.

8. Save and close the appointment.

Appointment Reminders

An appointment reminder is a visual and auditory alarm notifying you that you have an appointment. By default, each scheduled appointment has a reminder of 15 minutes.

Procedure Reference: Create a Recurring Appointment

To create a recurring appointment:

1. In the Date Navigator, select the date of the appointment.

2. On the Standard toolbar, click the New Appointment button to display a new Appointment form.

3. In the Subject field, enter a subject of your choice.

4. In the Location field, enter a location of your choice.

5. From the Start Time drop-down list, select the appropriate starting time of the appointment.

6. From the End Time drop-down list, select the appropriate ending time of the appointment.

7. On the Standard toolbar, click Recurrence to display the Appointment Recurrence dialog box.

8. If necessary, in the Recurrence Pattern box, select the recurrence pattern.

9. If necessary, in the Range Of Recurrence box, select the range of recurrence.
10. Click OK to close the dialog box and return to the Appointment form.
11. Save and close the appointment.

Procedure Reference: Create an Event

To create an event:

1. In the Date Navigator, select the date of the appointment.
2. On the Standard toolbar, click the New Appointment button to display a new Appointment form.
3. In the Subject field, enter a subject of your choice.
4. In the Location field, enter a location of your choice.
5. Check the All Day Event check box.
6. From the End Time drop-down list, select the appropriate ending time of the appointment.
7. From the Show Time As drop-down list, select the desired option.
8. Save and close the appointment.

TOPIC C

Assign a Category to an Appointment

You have added several business and personal appointments to your Calendar. It would be great if there was a way to quickly identify which appointments were the most important. In this topic, you will assign a category to an appointment.

Your Calendar contains some appointments that you don't want to miss, such as your performance appraisal. It also contains some appointments that you would like to miss, such as lunch with your co-worker whom you despise. By organizing your appointments so that similar appointments are grouped together, it will be easy to identify the appointments you don't want to miss.

Category

Definition:

A *category* is a keyword or phrase that you can assign to related items so that you can easily track the items.

Example:

Figure 4-4 displays an example of default categories in Outlook.

Lesson 4

Figure 4-4: *The default categories.*

How to Assign a Category to an Appointment

Procedure Reference: Assign a Category to an Existing Appointment

To assign a category to an existing appointment:

📌 You can assign a category while you're creating an appointment.

1. Open the appointment to which you want to assign a category.
   - Double-click the appointment.
   - Right-click the appointment and choose Open.
   - Select the appointment and choose File→Open→Selected Items.
2. Click Categories to display the Categories dialog box.
3. In the Available Categories list box, check the category to which you want to assign the appointment.
4. Click OK.
5. Save and close the appointment.

Procedure Reference: Assign a Category to a Recurring Appointment

To assign a category to a recurring appointment:

1. Open the appointment to which you want to assign a category.
   - Double-click the appointment.
   - Right-click the appointment and choose Open.
   - Select the appointment and choose File→Open→Selected Items.
2. In the Open Recurring Item dialog box, click OK.

3. Click Categories to display the Categories dialog box.

4. In the Available Categories list box, check the category to which you want to assign the appointment.

5. Click OK.

6. Save and close the appointment.

TOPIC D

Update Calendar Entries

You have just scheduled some appointments in your Calendar. What if the date, time, or location of an appointment changes? In this topic, you will update Calendar entries.

It never fails—the minute you schedule an appointment, you learn about another one you have to attend that's scheduled for the same time. When you're done crossing out, filling in, whiting out, or erasing your appointment information, your paper-based calendar is a mess. By using the Outlook Calendar, you can throw away your eraser and correction fluid. Updating your Calendar is a breeze, and your Calendar remains neat and organized, ensuring accurate appointment information.

How to Update Calendar Entries

Procedure Reference: Edit Appointments

To edit an appointment:

1. Open the Appointment form of the appointment that you want to edit.

2. Make the appropriate edits in the Appointment form.

3. Click Save And Close.

Delete Appointments

There are a few options for deleting an appointment. To delete an appointment, you can:

- Right-click the appointment and choose Delete.
- Select the appointment and on the Standard toolbar, click the Delete button.
- Open the appointment and on the Standard toolbar, click the Delete button.

LESSON 4

Lesson 4 Follow-up

Nice work! Now you know how to use the Calendar to keep track of all your appointments and events. You can schedule an appointment at a specified time, assign a category to an appointment, and update Calendar entries. Now your schedule will always be up-to-date and easy to read.

1. **What are some functions that you can perform by using the Outlook Calendar that you cannot perform with a paper-based calendar?**

    Answers will vary.

2. **When scheduling appointments, will you use categories? Why or why not?**

    Answers will vary.

LESSON 5
Scheduling Meetings

Lesson Time
60 minutes to 70 minutes

In this lesson, you will schedule meetings.

You will:

- Schedule a meeting.
- Reply to a meeting request.
- Propose a new meeting time.
- Track meeting responses.
- Update a meeting request.
- Cancel a meeting request.
- Print the Calendar.

Lesson 5

Introduction

You have used the Inbox to send messages and the Calendar to track your important appointments. In this lesson, you will combine these two tasks to schedule and coordinate meetings that involve multiple participants.

You need to schedule a department meeting. You must notify all employees, reserve a slide projector, and determine who will be attending. By using Outlook, you can electronically communicate and track attendance of participants and resources at meetings from one central location.

Topic A

Schedule a Meeting

When you scheduled appointments that involved your schedule only, all you had to do was enter the information in your Calendar. Now, you will combine two of the tasks you've already learned—sending mail messages and scheduling appointments—to schedule meetings that involve multiple participants.

You need to schedule a department meeting. You could invite the participants by phone, but that will take some time, especially if someone is not available at the designated time. By scheduling a meeting in Outlook, you can quickly invite the appropriate participants and resources all at the same time, and you can pick a time that is available for everyone.

The Meeting Scheduling Process

The process begins with a Meeting form that you complete and send to all the meeting participants. The meeting is scheduled on your Calendar as soon as you send the Meeting form. As each participant accepts or tentatively accepts the meeting, it is inserted on their Calendar, and a response is sent to the meeting organizer. If the meeting is declined or a new time is proposed, a reply is sent. Figure 5-1 displays the meeting scheduling process.

Lesson 5

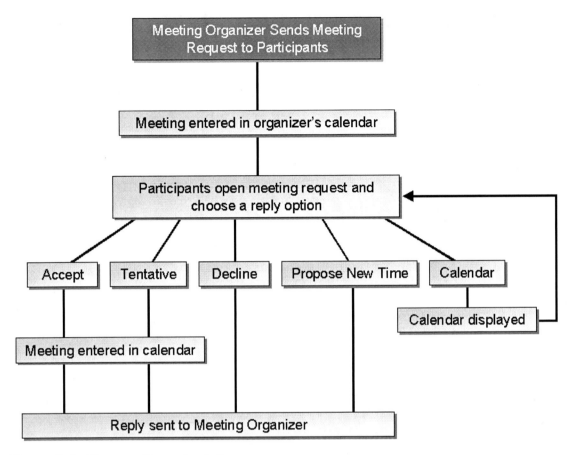

Figure 5-1: *The meeting scheduling process.*

The Meeting Form

The Meeting form is used to invite participants to a meeting. It consists of three tabs:
- The *Appointment* tab allows you to enter a subject, a location for the meeting, start and end times, and any other information regarding the meeting.
- The *Scheduling* tab allows you to coordinate the meeting to fit the schedules of all attendees.
- The *Tracking* tab displays the meeting participants and their replies. This section is not visible until the Meeting form is sent to the participants.

Figure 5-2 displays an example of a completed Meeting form.

Lesson 5

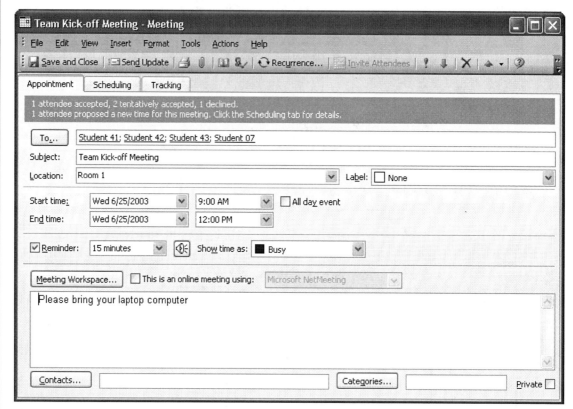

Figure 5-2: *A completed Meeting form.*

Meeting Resources

Definition:

A *meeting resource* is an item with its own email account on the Microsoft Exchange Server that you can schedule for a meeting, and it will automatically accept or reject meeting invitations.

Example:

Figure 5-3 displays examples of meeting resources in the Global Address List.

Lesson 5

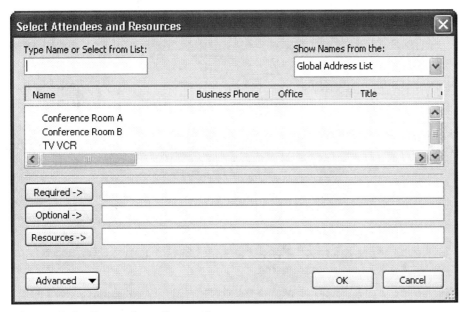

Figure 5-3: *Examples of meeting resources.*

How to Schedule a Meeting

Procedure Reference: Schedule a Meeting

To schedule a meeting:

1. In the Date Navigator, select the date of the meeting.

2. In the Appointment section, click the time you want the meeting to start.

    > You can also select the date and time in the Meeting form.

3. On the Standard toolbar, click the New Appointment button drop-down arrow and choose Meeting Request to display a new Meeting form.

4. To address the request by using the Global Address List, click To to display the Select Attendees And Resources dialog box.

    > You can also type the user names of the attendees directly in the To text box, separating each user name with a semicolon (;).

5. In the list box, select the appropriate attendees.

6. Click Required to add the selected user names to the Required text box.

7. If necessary, in the list box, select the appropriate resources.

8. If necessary, click Resources to add the selected resources to the Resources text box.

9. Click OK to return to the Meeting form.

10. In the Subject text box, enter a meeting subject.

11. If necessary, from the End Time drop-down list, select an end time for the meeting.

Lesson 5: Scheduling Meetings 45

Lesson 5

12. To check the availability of the attendees, select the Scheduling tab.
13. On the Standard toolbar, click Send to send the meeting request.

Online Meetings

To schedule an online meeting:

1. Open and complete a Meeting form as you would if you were scheduling an in-person meeting.
2. Check the This Is An Online Meeting Using check box and from the accompanying drop-down list, select one of the options.
   - Microsoft NetMeeting
   - Windows Media Services
   - Microsoft Exchange Conferencing
3. If you are using Microsoft NetMeeting, in the Directory Server text box, enter the name of the server you are using.
4. If you are using Windows Media Services, in the Event Address text box, enter the address of the event.
5. If you are using Microsoft Exchange Conferencing:
   - If you want to create a private meeting, uncheck the Allow External Attendees Or Users Without Trusted User Certificates To Join The Conference check box.
   - If you want to require a password for those entering the meeting, in the Password text box, enter a password.
6. If you want a Microsoft NetMeeting or a Windows Media Services broadcast to start automatically, check the appropriate option.
   - Automatically Start NetMeeting With Reminder
   - Automatically Start Windows Media With Reminder
7. Click Send.

Lesson 5

Topic B

Reply to a Meeting Request

You know how to schedule a meeting and invite participants to your meeting. But how do you respond to an invitation to someone else's meeting? In this topic, you will reply to a meeting request.

You received a meeting invitation from a co-worker. You could call her and tell her that you will be attending, but what if she (or you) forgets to document your participation? By using Outlook to reply to a meeting request, the meeting chairperson will be assured of your attendance. Therefore, you won't have to worry about showing up for a meeting at which your attendance isn't expected. Also, you won't forget about the meeting because it will be documented on your electronic Calendar.

How to Reply to a Meeting Request

Procedure Reference: Reply to a Meeting Request

To accept or decline a meeting request:

1. In the Inbox, open the meeting request message.
2. If desired, on the Standard toolbar, click Calendar to check your Calendar.
3. If necessary, click the Close button to close the Calendar.
4. Accept or decline a meeting request.
   - To accept the meeting request.
     a. On the Standard toolbar, click Accept.
     b. In the message box, click OK to send the response.

   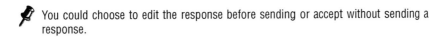
   You could choose to edit the response before sending or accept without sending a response.

   - To decline the meeting request.
     a. On the Standard toolbar, click Decline. A message box is displayed.
     b. Click OK to edit the response before sending.
     c. In the message area of the response form, type a response.
     d. Click OK.

   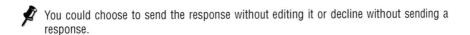
   You could choose to send the response without editing it or decline without sending a response.

5. Click Send.

Meeting Conflicts

When you open a meeting request for a meeting that conflicts with another appointment on your Calendar, Outlook alerts you by displaying a warning in the InfoBar. Conflicting meetings are displayed adjacent to each other on the Calendar.

Lesson 5: Scheduling Meetings

Lesson 5

Topic C

Propose a New Meeting Time

You have seen how to accept and decline a meeting request. However, what if you need to attend a meeting but are not available at the requested date or time? In this topic, you will discover how to propose a new meeting time.

You received an invitation to a meeting which you need to attend, but you are not available at the scheduled time. You could decline the invitation and compose a new message suggesting an alternate meeting time and requesting the meeting chairperson's reply; however, that will take some time and possibly a lot of emails. To save time, you could propose a new time for the meeting.

How to Propose a New Meeting Time

Procedure Reference: Propose a New Meeting Time

To propose a new meeting time:

1. In the Inbox, open the meeting request message.
2. On the Standard toolbar, click Propose New Time to display the Propose New Time dialog box.
3. From the Meeting Start Time drop-down list, select a new time.
4. Click Propose Time to display the Meeting Response form.
5. In the message text box, enter a response.
6. Click Send.

Topic D

Track Meeting Responses

You have received meeting replies for various meetings you have scheduled. What do you do when you need to determine who will be attending those meetings? In this topic, you will track meeting responses.

You have a department meeting scheduled for tomorrow. You need to determine exactly how many people will be attending so that you can prepare the handouts. By using Outlook, you can quickly track who has responded and who has not responded to a meeting request.

How to Track Meeting Responses

Procedure Reference: Track Meeting Responses

To track meeting responses:

1. Display the Calendar.

Lesson 5

2. Display the date on which the meeting is scheduled.
3. Double-click the meeting to open it.
4. Select the Tracking tab.
5. Click the Close button to close the Meeting form.

TOPIC E

Update a Meeting Request

You have created a number of meeting requests. What if you discover that you need to change the location or time of one of those meetings? In this topic, you will update a meeting request.

You scheduled a meeting on the wrong day. You intended for the meeting to be on a Monday rather than a Tuesday. You could send cancellation notices and new meeting invites, but that will require a lot of work on your part and generate a lot of mail for all the attendees of the meeting. An easier and quicker solution is to reschedule the meeting by updating the meeting request.

How to Update a Meeting Request

Procedure Reference: Update a Meeting Request

To update a meeting request:

1. In the Calendar, open the Meeting form.
2. Make the appropriate changes to the Meeting form.
3. Send the update.
   a. If you want to notify attendees of the changes, on the Standard toolbar, click the Send Update To Attendees And Close button.
   b. If you don't need to notify the attendees of the changes, on the Standard toolbar, click Save And Close.

Lesson 5: Scheduling Meetings

LESSON 5

TOPIC F

Cancel a Meeting Request

You scheduled a meeting and edited meeting details. You also accepted meetings. Priorities change and emergencies happen so it's inevitable that schedules need to be adjusted. In this topic, you will cancel a meeting and notify attendees of the cancellation.

You have a meeting scheduled for tomorrow. A large number of participants are attending. You have a conflict, so you're going to have to cancel the meeting. You don't have time to call everyone. Luckily, you can use Outlook to quickly solve your problem. When you cancel a meeting in Outlook, each participant is automatically notified. Therefore, you won't have to worry about a participant showing up for a meeting that has been cancelled. In addition, participants' Calendars will be clear so they can attend other potential meetings instead.

How to Cancel a Meeting Request

Procedure Reference: Cancel a Meeting

To cancel a meeting:

1. In the Calendar, select the meeting entry that you want to cancel.

2. On the Standard toolbar, click Delete. A message box is displayed. The option to send a cancellation message and delete the meeting is selected.

   You can also delete a meeting without sending a cancellation message.

3. Click OK. A Meeting form is displayed.

4. If desired, in the Meeting form, enter a message.

5. Click Send to send the cancellation message.

TOPIC G

Print the Calendar

Now that you have created and modified several Calendar entries, your Calendar is up to date. What if you want to carry a hard copy of your appointments with you? In this topic, you will print the Calendar.

You are going to be out of the office on business. You have a number of meetings scheduled while you are away, but you won't have your computer with you. By printing a copy of your Calendar before you leave, you will know what your schedule is while you are away, and you won't have to worry about missing a meeting.

How to Print the Calendar

Procedure Reference: Print the Calendar

To print the Calendar:

1. With the Calendar open, on the Standard toolbar, click the Print button to display the Print dialog box.
2. From the Print Style list box, select a Calendar style.
3. In the Print Range box, specify the start date to designate the start time that you want printed.
4. In the Print Range box, specify the end date to designate the end time that you want printed.
5. If necessary, select other print options.
6. If desired, click Preview to display Print Preview.
7. If desired, click to zoom in.
8. If necessary, click Print to return to the Print dialog box.
9. Click OK to print the Calendar.

Lesson 5 Follow-up

Great job! The task of organizing meetings has now been greatly simplified for you. You can use Outlook to organize meetings that involve any number of participants. You can use information available from their Calendars to schedule a meeting at a time that will work for all participants. You know how to keep track of who is coming to a meeting and who hasn't responded yet. When you receive a meeting request, you can send a reply to the meeting organizer. If you have to cancel a meeting, you know how to do it so that all participants are immediately notified of the cancellation.

1. What were some things you had to take care of the last time you scheduled a meeting that would have been easier to do through the Calendar?

    Answers will vary.

2. Have you ever tentatively agreed to a meeting? What were your reasons for tentatively accepting rather than accepting?

Lesson 5

Answers will vary.

LESSON 6
Managing Contacts

Lesson Time
40 minutes to 50 minutes

In this lesson, you will manage contacts and contact information.

You will:

- Add a contact to the Outlook Address Book.
- Sort contacts.
- Find a contact.
- Generate a map to a contact's location.
- Edit a contact's information.
- Delete a contact.
- Print a list of contacts.

Lesson 6

Introduction

You used the Inbox to send and receive messages, and you used the Calendar to schedule and cancel appointments and meetings—all with people within your organization. In this lesson, you will use the Contacts section to keep track of contacts outside of your organization.

You have quite a collection of business cards; however, that fax number you need in a hurry always seems hard to find. Outlook makes it easy to organize all the information you need about your business and personal associates. Names, addresses, and phone numbers are easily searchable and easy to retrieve and update.

Topic A

Add a Contact

Many of the tasks you've completed in Outlook have involved people within your organization. In the course of your workday, you have frequent interactions with people outside your organization, and they all have pieces of information, such as addresses, email addresses, work numbers, cell phone numbers, and fax numbers of which to keep track. In this topic, you will use the Contact section to help you keep track of all that information.

You send frequent mail messages to George Messerschmidt, a key client. Because he does not work for your company, his email address is not in the Global Address List. Every time you send him a message, you have to type his email address, which is georgemesserschmidt@msmoveandstore.com. Several times now you've misspelled the email address and the message bounced back to you as undeliverable. By adding George's email address to Outlook once, you can quickly retrieve it whenever you need it, saving typing time and avoiding misspellings and undeliverable messages.

Contacts

Definition:

A *contact* is a person with whom you communicate on a business or personal level and whose personal or business (or both) information is stored in the Contacts folder.

Example:

Figure 6-1 displays an example of a contact.

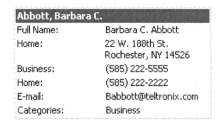

Figure 6-1: *An example of a contact.*

Lesson 6

The Contact Form

When you create a new contact, Outlook displays a Contact form that contains tabs and text boxes in which you can enter personal and business information.

Figure 6-2 displays an example of a completed Contact form.

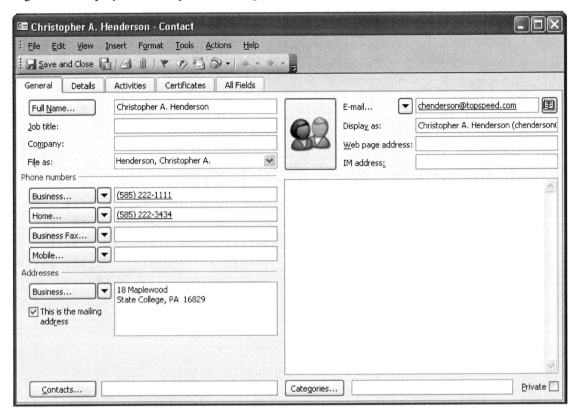

Figure 6-2: *A completed Contact form.*

The Outlook Address Book

Definition:

The *Outlook Address Book* is a list that contains all contacts that you create by using the Contact form.

Example:

Figure 6-3 displays the contents of an Outlook Address Book.

Lesson 6: Managing Contacts

Lesson 6

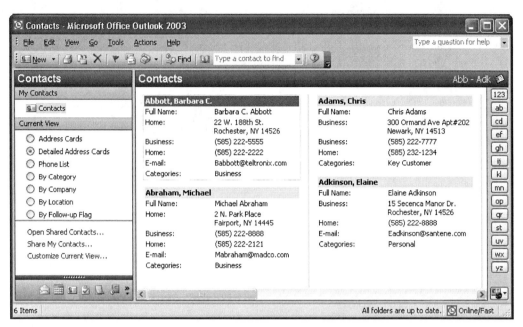

Figure 6-3: *The contents of an Outlook Address Book.*

How to Add a Contact

Procedure Reference: Add a Contact

To add a contact to the Outlook Address Book:

1. On the Go Menu, select Contacts to display the contents of the Contacts folder.
2. Display a new Contact form.
   - On the Standard toolbar, click the New Contact button.
   - Right-click and choose New Contact.
   - Choose File→New→Contact.
   - Choose Actions→New Contact.
3. Enter the desired information in the appropriate text boxes.
4. If desired, assign a contact to a category.
   a. Click Categories to display the Categories dialog box.
   b. In the Available Categories list box, check the appropriate category.
   c. Click OK.
5. On the Standard toolbar, click Save And Close.

Topic B

Sort Contacts

Your Outlook Address Book contains many contacts. What if you need to quickly display the contact information for all your business associates in a particular state? In this topic, you will sort contacts.

Outlook contains over 75 contacts for a particular client. You want to invite all of those contacts to an upcoming presentation. You printed your contact list, but it's in alphabetical order by name, so it's going to take time to locate all the employees for that one company. By sorting your contact list by company, you can quickly locate the names and addresses of all the contacts you want to invite to the presentation.

Sort Order

Definition:

Sort order is the sequence in which items are arranged.

Example:

Examples of different sort orders include:

- Ascending—A-Z
- Descending—Z-A

Figure 6-4 displays examples of contacts that are sorted in ascending and descending order.

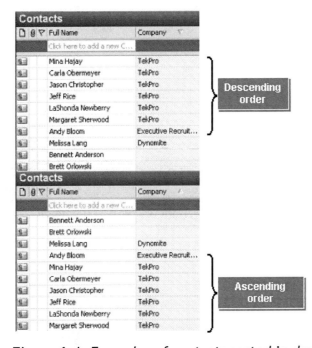

Figure 6-4: *Examples of contacts sorted in descending and ascending order.*

Lesson 6: Managing Contacts

Lesson 6

How to Sort Contacts

Procedure Reference: Sort Contacts

To sort contacts:

1. Click any column header to sort by that header title. A small triangle to the right of the column name indicates that the list has been sorted by that column in a particular order.

2. Click the column header a second time to sort that column in reverse order.

 You can sort mail messages by using the View menu.

Topic C

Find a Contact

You added contacts and their information to the Contacts section. But having all that information is only useful if you can retrieve it quickly and efficiently. In this topic, you will find contact information.

You need to call a client. You know the name of his company, but you can't remember his name. By using Outlook's search feature, you can quickly locate the information for the client you need to contact by entering his company name.

How to Find a Contact

Procedure Reference: Find a Contact

To find a contact:

1. In the Find A Contact text box, click to activate the text box.

2. Type the name, company name, or other text on which you're going to search.

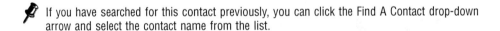 If you have searched for this contact previously, you can click the Find A Contact drop-down arrow and select the contact name from the list.

3. Press Enter to display any contacts that match the word(s) you entered.

Searchable Terms

When you enter a word or phrase in the Find A Contact text box, Outlook looks in the Contact folder for a word or phrase that matches. By default, Outlook only searches for partial names, first or last names, email addresses, display as names, and company names.

Microsoft® Office Outlook® 2003– Level 1

Topic D

Generate a Map

You added a number of contacts and you've seen how easy it is to find specific information about a contact. Now, you need to travel to a specific contact's location. In this topic, you will generate a map.

You have a meeting scheduled with a client at the client's location. You have the address, but you don't know how to get there. By using Outlook, you can quickly generate a map. You won't have to worry about being late for the meeting because you got lost.

How to Generate a Map

Procedure Reference: Generate a Map

To generate a map to a contact:

1. If necessary, display the Contact form of the contact for which you want to generate a map.

2. If necessary, from the Addresses drop-down list, select the address you want to map.

    You can generate a map to the address of any contact located in the United States.

3. On the Standard toolbar, click the Display Map Of Address button. A map to the contact's location is displayed in Internet Explorer.

4. If desired, click as needed to zoom in to the address on the map.

5. In the Internet Explorer window, click the Close button.

6. In the Contact form, click the Close button.

LESSON 6

TOPIC E

Edit a Contact

After you create and work with your contacts, you discover that some of the contact information has changed. In this topic, you will edit a contact.

Contact information changes frequently. Whether it's an updated address or phone number, you know what a hassle it is to cross out (or white out) information in your address book and squeeze in new information. Outlook puts an end to messy address books or card files. Your contact information will be neat and easy to read. You won't have to worry about dialing an incorrect phone number, because you misread a sloppy, handwritten number.

How to Edit a Contact

Procedure Reference: Edit a Contact

To edit a contact's information:

1. Open the Contact form that you want to edit.
    - Double-click the Contact.
    - Select the contact and choose File→Open→Selected Items.
    - Right-click the contact and choose Open.
2. Edit the appropriate information.
3. Click Save And Close.

TOPIC F

Delete a Contact

You have some contact information that you no longer use. In this topic, you will delete a contact.

Your address book contains a number of contacts with whom you no longer do business. By deleting those old contacts, your address book will be less cluttered and you will save space on your hard drive.

How to Delete a Contact

Procedure Reference: Delete a Contact

There are a few different options for deleting a contact.

1. Delete a contact.
    - Select the contact, and on the Standard toolbar, click the Delete button.
    - Right-click the contact and choose Delete.

- Select the contact and choose Edit→Delete.

TOPIC G
Print Contacts

Contact information is very useful when stored on your PC. However, what if you travel a lot and can't always access your contact information? In this topic, you will print contacts.

You will be out of the office on business. While you are away, you will be meeting with a number of contacts whose information is stored in your address book. You won't have your computer with you. By printing your contact list before you leave, you will have the appropriate information with you, so you can easily call or visit a contact.

How to Print Contacts

Procedure Reference: Print Contacts

To print contact information:

1. On the Standard toolbar, click the Print button to display the Print dialog box.
2. From the Print Style list box, select a print style.
3. If necessary, select other print options.
4. If desired, click Preview to display Print Preview.
5. If desired, click to zoom in.
6. If necessary, click Print to return to the Print dialog box.
7. Click OK to print the contacts.

Lesson 6 Follow-up

Good work! You can now replace your messy rotary card file with a much more efficient system of storing information. You know how to create and maintain a contact list and how to access and view the list and individual contact information. You also know how to sort and find contacts and generate a map to a contact.

1. **What are some things that you frequently look up in your rotary card file that would be useful to store in the Outlook Contacts section?**

    Answers will vary.

2. **What are some custom category names that you could create to help you organize your contacts?**

    Answers will vary.

Notes

LESSON 7
Managing Tasks

Lesson Time
20 minutes to 30 minutes

In this lesson, you will create and edit tasks.

You will:

- Create a task.
- Edit a task.
- Update a task.

Lesson 7

Introduction

Communicating with messages, scheduling appointments and meetings, and organizing contact information are some common office procedures that you can accomplish with Outlook. You can also keep track of tasks by using Outlook. In this lesson, you will create and edit tasks, as well as mark them complete when they are done.

You are in the middle of writing a message and you think of something else that needs to be done. You could scribble yourself a note, hoping that it doesn't get lost in the shuffle. A better option is to enter the task in Outlook. Then, you will always have an electronic reminder of what needs to be done and when.

Topic A

Create a Task

Sometimes you might want to create a reminder for yourself about a project that doesn't need to go on your Calendar and you want to track its progress. In this topic, you will create a task.

When you schedule an appointment or meeting in Outlook, by default you are reminded about the appointment or meeting 15 minutes before the scheduled time. Similar to appointments and meetings, if you have tasks you need to accomplish, you can be reminded of those tasks by documenting them in Outlook. Then, you will have an electronic list of what you need to do and when you need to do it.

Task

Definition:

A *task* is an assigned piece of work that must be completed within a certain time frame.

Example:

Figure 7-1 displays some examples of tasks.

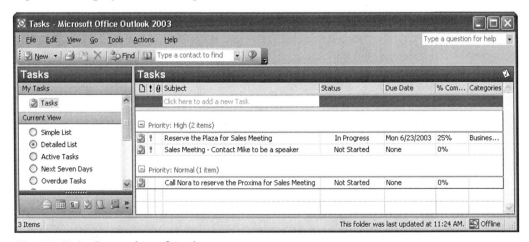

Figure 7-1: *Examples of tasks.*

The Task Form

The Task form contains the Task and Details tabs on which you can enter information for a task. Figure 7-2 displays an example of a completed Task Form.

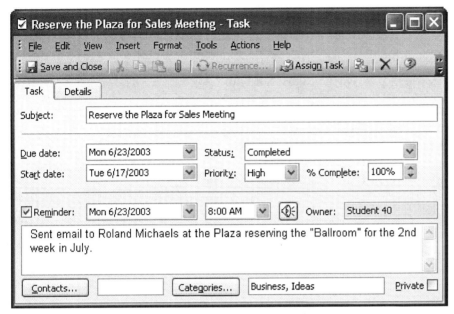

Figure 7-2: *An example of a completed Task Form.*

Task Form Options

Table 7-1 lists and describes some of the text boxes in the Task form.

Table 7-1: *Task Form Options*

Text Box	Description
Status	Displays one of five status choices: • Not Started • In Progress • Completed • Waiting On Someone Else • Deferred
Priority	Low, Normal, High.
% Complete	How far along on the task you are.
Note area	Any additional notes about the task.
Categories	You can assign a category to a task.
Total Work	Used for entering the estimated hours.
Actual Hours	Used for entering the actual hours.
Companies	Used for entering companies which you need to bill for services.

Lesson 7: Managing Tasks

Lesson 7

How to Create a Task

Procedure Reference: Create a Task

To create a task:

1. If necessary, display the Tasks list.
2. On the Standard toolbar, click the New Task button to display a new Task form.
3. In the Subject text box, enter a subject of your choice.
4. From the Due Date pop-up Calendar, select the date when the task is due.

   You can type Today, Tomorrow, or enter a date in the Due Date text box.

5. If necessary, from the Priority drop-down list, select a priority.
6. If necessary, from the Reminder pop-up Calendar, select a date when you want to be reminded of the task.
7. On the Standard toolbar, click Save And Close.

Topic B

Edit a Task

You have entered information for an upcoming task. But like everything else, tasks are liable to change. In this topic, you will make some changes to the task by updating previously entered information.

You created a task to complete the monthly slide show presentation by Friday. Your manager tells you it needs to be completed a day earlier. You could create a new task, but it would be easier to edit the existing task. You can quickly edit the date of the task, ensuring that the task information is accurate.

How to Edit a Task

Procedure Reference: Edit a Task

To edit a task:

1. If necessary, display the Tasks list.
2. Open the task you want to edit.
3. Make the appropriate changes to the Task form.
4. Save and close the Task form.

TOPIC C

Update a Task

You have entered a task and edited information about the task. What do you do with a task item when you are finished? In this topic, you will indicate that a task has been completed.

You have completed the monthly slide show presentation. You want to indicate that on the task list. By updating the status of the task, it will display as complete, making it easy for you to quickly track the progress of that task or any other task on the list.

How to Update a Task

Procedure Reference: Update a Task

To update a task:

1. If necessary, display the Tasks list.
2. In the Complete column, check the check box of the task you have completed. The task is marked as completed and is crossed off.

Lesson 7 Follow-up

Well done! Getting organized is critical to accomplishing tasks efficiently. You now know how to create tasks so that you know, at a glance, everything you have to accomplish. You also know how to edit tasks so that they are always up-to-date, as well as how to update a task once you're done.

1. **How could a task list help you accomplish your job more efficiently?**

    Answers will vary.

2. **When you are working on a project, what kinds of information do you have to keep track of that could be stored in the task list?**

    Answers will vary.

Notes

LESSON 8
Using Notes

In this lesson, you will create and edit notes.

You will:

- Create a note.
- Edit a note.
- Move a note.

Lesson Time
20 minutes to 30 minutes

LESSON 8

Introduction

So far, you've seen how a number of Outlook components can help you work more efficiently. Another common task you probably do regularly is make notes to yourself, so that you don't forget something. Wouldn't it be nice if you could do this electronically? In this lesson, you will create, edit, and move notes.

You have paper notes with writing scattered all over your desk. What if you misplace or accidentally throw away one of those notes? Instead, you can use Outlook to electronically store your thoughts and ideas as notes and easily reference or update those notes whenever needed.

TOPIC A

Create a Note

In Outlook, you have a place for everything. You can communicate by using the Inbox and schedule appointments and meetings in the Calendar. You can store information about business and personal contacts and keep track of tasks. What if you need to jot down an idea or thought? In this topic, you will use notes to do that.

While composing a message, you think of an issue you want bring up at the next department meeting. You could stop what you're doing and work on the meeting item, but you really want to complete the message first. By using Outlook, you can quickly document your thoughts and ideas for easy reference later. You won't have to worry about misplacing your thoughts and ideas that you scribbled on a piece of paper.

How to Create a Note

Procedure Reference: Create a Note

To create a note:

1. In the Navigation Pane on the Quick Launch bar, click the Notes button to display the Notes folder.
2. On the Standard toolbar, click the New Note button to display a new note.
3. Enter the contents of the note.
4. If necessary, assign the note to a category.
    a. Click the Note icon and choose Categories to display the Categories dialog box.
    b. From the Available Categories list box, check the category to which you want to assign the note.
    c. Click OK.
5. If necessary, place the mouse pointer on the resizing handle until a double-headed arrow is displayed and drag to resize the note.
6. Click the Close button to close the note.

Topic B

Edit a Note

After you create a note, you might want to add or delete information from that note. In this topic, you will edit the contents of a note.

You created a note for an issue that you want to discuss at the next department meeting. You have been thinking about the issue, and you want to jot down additional thoughts and ideas. By editing an existing note, you ensure that your thoughts and ideas are accurately documented and related information will be stored in the same place.

How to Edit a Note

Procedure Reference: Edit a Note

To edit a note:

1. If necessary, display the Notes folder.
2. Open the note you want to edit by using one of the following methods:
   - If the note is selected, press Enter.
   - Double-click the note.
   - Right-click the note and choose Open.
3. Edit the contents of the note as desired.
4. If necessary, resize the note.
5. Close the note.

Topic C

Copy a Note

You created a note and edited it. To be more organized, you want the note to display in a different location. In this topic, you will copy a note.

You have captured a number of ideas relating to an issue you want to discuss at the next department meeting. You don't want to forget to mention the issue at the scheduled time. By copying the note to your desktop, the issue will be visible as soon as you log in the morning of the meeting, reminding you that you want to discuss the issue.

How to Copy a Note

Procedure Reference: Copy a Note

To copy a note to the desktop:

1. If necessary, display the Notes folder.

Lesson 8

2. Adjust the size of the Outlook window so that the desktop is visible.
3. Drag the note you want to copy to the desktop.

You can also copy or move a note to a folder.

Lesson 8 Follow-up

The Outlook Notes section allows you to capture those miscellaneous bits of information that you don't want to lose or forget. You know how to enter information into a note, edit a note, and move a note.

1. **What are some things that you frequently jot down on sticky notes that would be suitable for Outlook notes?**

    Answers will vary.

2. **How do you think using notes could be helpful to you in your job?**

    Answers will vary.

Follow-up

Congratulations! You've mastered the critical skills that you need to begin communicating by using Outlook 2003.

1. **Of the tools covered in this course, which one(s) will you use the most? Which one(s) will you use the least?**

2. **What do you feel is the biggest advantage of using Outlook 2003? Why? What is the biggest disadvantage of using Outlook 2003? Why?**

What's Next?

This course is the first in a series. After completing this course, students might be interested in expanding their knowledge of Microsoft® Outlook® 2003 by taking *Microsoft Outlook 2003 – Level 2* and *Microsoft Outlook 2003 – Level 3*.

Notes

APPENDIX A
Microsoft Office Specialist Program

Selected Element K courseware addresses Microsoft Office Specialist skills. The following tables indicate where Outlook® 2003 skills are covered. For example, 1-3 indicates the lesson and activity number applicable to that skill.

Core Skill Sets and Skills Being Measured	Outlook® 2003: Level 1	Outlook® 2003: Level 2	Outlook® 2003: Level 3
Originate and Respond to E-mail and Instant Messages			
Addressing e-mail messages and instant messages to recipients	1-3, 2-1		1-3
Forwarding and replying to e-mail messages and instant messages	1-5, 2-5		1-3
Attach Files to Items			
Inserting attachments to e-mail and instant messages	2-4		1-4
Create and Modify a Personal Signature for Message			
Creating and modifying e-mail signatures			2-3, 2-4, 2-5
Creating unique e-mail signatures for multiple accounts			2-3, 2-4
Modify E-mail Message Settings and Delivery Options			
Flagging e-mail messages	3-2		
Formatting e-mail messages (e.g., HTML, Rich Text, and Plain Text)		3-3	
Setting e-mail message importance and sensitivity		3-1	
Setting e-mail message delivery options		3-2	
Create and Edit Contacts			

Appendix A

Core Skill Sets and Skills Being Measured	Outlook® 2003: Level 1	Outlook® 2003: Level 2	Outlook® 2003: Level 3
Adding contacts and contact information to e-mail and Instant Messenger	6-1		1-2
Updating and modifying contact information	6-5		
Accept, Decline, and Delegate Tasks			
Accepting, declining, and delegating tasks		5-1, 5-2	
Create, Modify Appointments, Meetings, and Events			
Adding appointments to the calendar	4-2		
Scheduling meetings and inviting attendees	5-1		
Scheduling resources for meetings	5-1		
Scheduling events	4-4		
Update, Cancel, and Respond to Meeting Requests			
Accepting and declining meeting requests	5-2		
Proposing new meeting times	5-3		
Updating and cancelling meeting requests	5-5, 5-6		
Customize Calendar Settings			
Setting calendar options		2-2, 2-3	
Setting work days and times		2-1	
Create, Modify, and Assign Tasks			
Creating, modifying, and assigning tasks	7-1, 7-2, 7-3	5-1	
Create and Modify Distribution Lists			
Creating and modifying distribution lists		3-5, 3-6	
Link Contacts to Other Items			
Tracking activities for contacts			4-5
Create and Modify Notes			
Creating and editing notes	8-1, 8-2		
Organize Items			
Adding and deleting fields			6-1
Sorting items	6-2	7-1	
Filtering messages		7-4	
Organizing items using colors, rules, and views	4-5, 6-2	7-5, 7-6, 7-7	3-3, 3-4
Organize Items Using Folders			
Creating and deleting folders for items	3-3, 3-6		

APPENDIX A

Core Skill Sets and Skills Being Measured	Outlook® 2003: Level 1	Outlook® 2003: Level 2	Outlook® 2003: Level 3
Moving items between folders	3-4, 3-5		
Archiving items			5-2
Search for Items			
Finding items	6-3	7-2, 7-3	
Using Search folders			3-2
Save Items in Different File Formats			
Saving items in different file formats (e.g., .htm or .txt)			5-1
Assign Items to Categories			
Assigning items to categories	6-1, 8-1		
Preview and Print Items			
Previewing and printing items	1-6, 5-7, 6-7		

Notes

GLOSSARY

Address Book
A collection of address books or address lists that you can use to find and select names, email addresses, and distribution lists to quickly address messages.

Appointment Section
A section of the Calendar that displays your schedule for one day in specified time slots.

attachment
A copy of any type of file or an Outlook item that you can add to an Outlook item and then separate from the Outlook item.

category
A keyword or phrase that you can assign to related items so that you can easily track the items.

contact
A person with whom you communicate on a business or personal level and whose information is stored in the Contacts folder.

Date Navigator
A section of the Calendar, displayed as two adjacent months, that you can use to navigate in the Calendar.

email
An application that allows a user to create, send, and receive electronic messages.

email address
A string used to specify the user name and the location where users can send you email.

folder
A tool that you can use to store and organize Outlook items.

Global Address List
A list of all user names and global distribution lists in a particular organization that is created and maintained by the Microsoft Exchange Server Administrator.

InfoBar
Displays information about what has occurred or what action you need to take, and is displayed below the active toolbar.

item
A basic element created in Outlook that holds information and is stored in a specific location.

meeting resource
An item with its own email account on the Microsoft Exchange Server that you can schedule for a meeting, and it will automatically accept or reject meeting invitations.

Net etiquette (Network etiquette)
Proper guidelines users should follow when communicating electronically across a network.

Outlook Address Book
A list that contains all contacts that you create by using the Contact form.

sort order
The sequence in which items are arranged.

spamming
The act of sending unsolicited advertisements to email recipients or newsgroups.

task
An assigned piece of work that you do regularly or just once that must be completed within a certain time frame.

GLOSSARY

view
A way to display items in an Outlook folder.

INDEX

A

Address Book, 18
Appointment forms, 34
appointments
  assigning a category to, 38
  deleting, 39
  editing, 39
  recurring, 36
  reminders, 36
  scheduling, 36
attachments, 22
  opening, 26
  saving, 26
AutoCorrect, 20

C

Calendar
  Appointment Section, 33
  Date Navigator, 33
  entries, 32
  printing, 51
  symbols, 35
  views, 33
category, 37
Contact form, 55
contacts, 54
  adding, 56
  deleting, 60
  editing, 60
  finding, 58
  printing, 61
  sorting, 58

E

email, 8
email address, 9
emoticons, 11
  Also See: smileys
events
  creating, 37

F

files
  attaching, 23
  size, 22
  type, 22
flaming, 11
folders, 6
  creating, 28
  deleting, 30

G

Global Address List, 19
grammar checking, 21

H

Help, 8

I

InfoBar, 13
item, 5

M

maps
  generating, 59
Meeting form, 43
meeting requests
  accepting, 47
  declining, 47
meeting resource, 44
meetings
  canceling, 50
  conflicts, 47
  online, 46
  proposing a new time, 48
  scheduling, 42
  tracking responses, 48
  updating requests, 49
Message forms, 9

Index

messages
  addressing, 19
  composing, 10
  copying to a folder, 29
  deleting, 15
  flagging, 27
  formatting, 20
  forwarding, 23
  marking unread, 27
  moving to folders, 28
  opening, 12
  printing, 14
  recalling, 21
  recovering deleted, 15
  replying to, 13
  saving, 12
  sending, 10
  symbols, 12

N

net etiquette, 10
notes
  copying, 71
  creating, 70
  editing, 71

O

Outlook
  components, 4
  logging on to, 3
Outlook Address Book, 55

S

smileys, 11
  Also See: emoticons
sort order, 57
spamming, 11
spell checking, 21

T

Task form, 65
tasks, 64
  creating, 66
  editing, 66
  updating, 67

V

views, 32

Classroom Learning — Applications Post-Event Survey

Instructor Name: _____ Course: _____ End Date: _____

Student Name: _____ Student E-mail Address: _____

Company _____ Job Role: _____

The quality of your experience is very important to us and your comments are an integral part of our quality control. Please take a moment to provide us with your observations. Thank you.

1. **What was your main objective for completing this training?**
   - ☐ Solve a particular problem
   - ☐ Prepare for a new product deployment or software upgrade
   - ☐ Build new skills and knowledge (not related to a new software deployment)
   - ☐ Prepare for a certification exam
   - ☐ Better understand products before purchasing new software
   - ☐ Prepare for a career change
   - ☐ Other (please specify) _____

2. **How would you rate this training on the following dimensions?**

Classroom
Extraordinary/Outstanding .... Unacceptable/Poor

Quality of the classroom environment	9 8 7 6 5	4 3 2 1
Performance of the technology used in the classroom (hardware/software)	9 8 7 6 5	4 3 2 1

Classroom Comments (if any) _____

Instructor
Extraordinary/Outstanding .... Unacceptable/Poor

Instructor's knowledge of the subject matter	9 8 7 6 5	4 3 2 1
Instructor's response to questions	9 8 7 6 5	4 3 2 1
Instructor's ability to provide real world experiences and examples	9 8 7 6 5	4 3 2 1
Instructor's presentation skills	9 8 7 6 5	4 3 2 1
Instructor's overall performance	9 8 7 6 5	4 3 2 1

Instructor Comments (if any) _____

Training Content
Extraordinary/Outstanding .... Unacceptable/Poor

Clarity of the training content	9 8 7 6 5	4 3 2 1
Flow of the training content	9 8 7 6 5	4 3 2 1
Depth of the training content	9 8 7 6 5	4 3 2 1
Effectiveness of the exercises in reinforcing the knowledge/skills learned	9 8 7 6 5	4 3 2 1
Relevance of the exercises to real world situations	9 8 7 6 5	4 3 2 1
Time dedicated to activities such as discussions, practices, and exercises (as opposed to lecture)	9 8 7 6 5	4 3 2 1
Language quality of the courseware (grammar, terminology, style)	9 8 7 6 5	4 3 2 1

How would you change the training content to improve your learning experience?
_____

Other training content comments (if any)
_____

3. **How would you rate this training on the following dimensions?**

   Learning Effectiveness
   Extraordinary/Outstanding .... Unacceptable/Poor

Knowledge and skills gained from this training	9 8 7 6 5	4 3 2 1
Impact of this training on your productivity related to the subject matter	9 8 7 6 5	4 3 2 1
	9 8 7 6 5	4 3 2 1

   Exceeded Expectations .... Did not meet expectations at all

4. **How well did this training meet your expectations?** 9 8 7 6 5 4 3 2 1

5. **Overall, how satisfied are you with this training?**
   ○ Very Satisfied   ○ Somewhat Satisfied   ○ Somewhat Dissatisfied   ○ Very Dissatisfied

6. **What percent of your total work time requires the knowledge/skills presented in this training? Check only one.**
   ☐0% ☐10% ☐20% ☐30% ☐40% ☐50% ☐60% ☐70% ☐80% ☐90% ☐100%

Applications Post-Event Survey

7. If you think this training will have a positive impact on your job performance, what areas will be impacted most? Check all that apply.
   - ☐ increasing quality
   - ☐ increasing ability to innovate
   - ☐ increasing customer satisfaction
   - ☐ increasing productivity
   - ☐ decreasing time to complete task(s)
   - ☐ increasing employee satisfaction
   - ☐ increasing sales
   - ☐ decreasing costs

8. Please indicate how much you expect your job performance related to the course subject matter to improve as a result this training and other business improvements in your organization.
   ☐0% ☐10% ☐20% ☐30% ☐40% ☐50% ☐60% ☐70% ☐80% ☐90% ☐100%

9. How much of the improvement in your job performance will be a direct result of this training? (For example if you feel that half of your improvement is a direct result of the training, enter 50% here.)
   ☐0% ☐10% ☐20% ☐30% ☐40% ☐50% ☐60% ☐70% ☐80% ☐90% ☐100%

10. **Would you like to be notified about advanced or complementary courses?**   ☐ Yes   ☐ No

Additional Questions   Strongly Agree   Strongly Disagree

11. My Account Executive/Educational Consultant is: _____
12. My Account Executive/Ed. Consultant has serviced my account satisfactorily   9 8 7 6 5 4 3 2 1
13. Is this your first time at New Horizons?   ○ Yes ○ No
14. Would you recommend New Horizons to others?   ○ Yes ○ No
15. Other classes you are interested in but not included in your learning plan: _____
16. Comments Suggestions to improve your experience?   _____

Thank you for completing the survey.

To make your own nameplate:

Remove this page from the book.
Print your name on the lines provided.
Fold as illustrated.

— FOLD HERE —

Print Your Name Here

— FOLD HERE —

Print Your Name Here